CW00539233

WORD/WORLD

WORD/WORLD

MARIANNE MORRIS

BOILER HOUSE PRESS

APPLES + ORIGINS

HOUSEKEEPING

In a house is the silence of what is a home.
We either keep a man out
or in, debate his sanity, might know
to stay away from one instinctively if
the colors have dark aureoles or if the color
of one is always smudged out
by the color of another, an ex for ex
ample, all wounds are ample,
knocking on the corners
of my head. At each edge I find
a little puddle of Lethe
to drop my crocodile toes in,
still expecting to be applauded
for my expert mockery, I guess that's
why I knew instinctively that a man would
not know the answer to my question: how
do you deal with female and female-
identified rage? But instead recommend
I read some other man and the other man
said "ridicule is MAN's most powerful weapon"
and I laughed but
underneath it I was really angry.

When I think of real death (as opposed to
just Lethe) it is unreal, which is how I know
there is something in this body that clings to me—
when I download the narrative
and insert it into my being, or when my legs
buckle from crying, or when I float on an
ember of my own making, home in the car
or when the car turns a city into a countryside
or when the wind whips my hair. Or when I see
how wrong I am, when singing whilst cooking,
when the land sprays up a pink tea tree or a

thistle bars the front porch or when a piece
of land has been untouched for a long time
beneath a canopy of fallen netting and dried pine
and the grass is high and dotted with lemon thyme
whose essence fills my nose because I throw
myself into it, crush it under my knees and elbows
and it breaks open and releases its oils—
then my feelings sit down at the feet of
what felt them. Sometimes all
you can do is wait—

Little by little we unstitch the soulmate
        from modern consciousness, understand
true connection as brief, and our natural
        movement as unfettered. But back then
I truly believed I could fantasmagorize
        you into using the telephone,
was wrong, tried to dominate, was late,
maybe it really is all about desire.
        I'm going home, like Frank,
except without any rue or melancholy.

I don't know about you but I am finding
        the fur rugs a little passé, like you
could use your machine differently,
        abandon archive. It's hard
                to go back to documents
                and favor desire over
                        having this body which
                does not know it.

Last week it was CONVINCED that the World Trade Center had been detonated by the US government. Fire aflame the face, horse nostrils, am I a host of nothing? So precious wandering. The morning has this intention behind it which is continually interrupted by my hand reaching for Internet, so long to those specific magical arrangements, drowned in exposure, but I am in the dark room, the light is so sparse, I've given up thinking about sex, the flowers are gone now but seeds arranged in their place, organised into symmetries, shake them out into the earth. Birds will be mad at me. But none of those flowers grow, know how to grow. The fact of things not going well is stamped out in a lung full of smoke, which wakes me in the early morning, before I am ready, and is dry, and is haunting. I think I have taught myself prosody, which means I have cut narrative out of myself like a hole, which reopens again and again at the doctor (9 different kinds of doctor 1) witch doctor, 2) plant doctor, 3) needles doctor, 4) other needles doctor, 5) speculum doctor, 6) DRUGS DOCTOR IS MY FAVORITE 7) judgy doctor, 8) intuitive doctor, 9) doctor underground). But each one of them has a story, just tells it either through me or against me, and the answer is going to be that I feel better, even when I don't, even when the wound reopens

There is more than one way to burn a witch. It's 1497. It's 2016. It's Europe. It's North America. It's oil. It's gas. It's something about how numb you have to be in order to care more about money, control, aggregation of power, power, profit, corporate expansion, tipping the balance, exploitation, rape, than the Earth that gave you life. How numb you have to be in order to only be able to escape tribal law through aggregation of the aforementioned, can only dream in paper green, can only rape your way to the top, can only exploit your way up, can only be a man, can only be a man, can only lie your way to the top, can only be a man, can only be a man, and the feminisms are a new war, can only be a man. Only a woman would. Only a man would. Only a woman would. Only a man would. A woman always. A woman never. A man always. A man never. Stop up your mouth. Swear to me you will never say never or always again. The new Earth is here. It is beautiful.

All the joints and fluid in them. All the bones. We named them. All the names. Insufficient in a language that separates. All the separations inadequate to describe the movement of dancing. All the steps split up into names. Rocks split up into names. The click of two rocks then they touch. The pillow a body resembles on a hot rock. The feel of a hot rock is not hard, a rock is hard, a body on a hot rock is neither a rock nor a body. A rock rocking on a rock in a hot sun between a rock and a body is not, water between rock between two rocks between the skin and the fabric is a body. Hot sun on a body on a hot rock is sun, is soft, is a body, is day, is time, is several birds playing. Sun on a hot rock makes the rock hotter. Foot on a hot rock makes the foot hotter. Sun on a rock on a river around a body is a soft, soft thing. Sun on a body on a rock on a river is a soft soft then a stumbling thing needing to move. A rock on its own in the sun is not on its own. No things are on their own. There are no things. No rocks, no bodies, no sun. There is a sun, there is a soft place, there is a soft wet place. It is under the stars, also it is of the stars, also it is above them, inside and above them. A hot rock a star an exploding sun, a wet body between cloth between rocks is drying. A wet body on a dry rock is a hot wet body drying. I feel like a wet seed wild in the ground. That seed that found ground. That seed that fell into hot ground. That seed in a slit. That seed tucked into a slit, split seed opened by moisture by earth by a sense of staying, by an urgency most solid. That seed most solid most splitting most mapped out splitting.

The world we had was asleep together, in a high up place with large, expansive windows. Every time I think I can get inside of you, it is this half-empty cave that coaxes, wood in the stove, just me in a dream curled around you in a dream, you the empty principle, you and me made a place that disappeared when time stopped / us from being in a field, in a forest, on a dark path of plants, no one wanted to share the light, I was afraid of the dark. How do I fill the empty principle, I fill it with these dates, these hopes, these unattainable cathected snakes, coil around my belly. I roll up the rug, kneel on it, and ask for your presence. I promise that I am happy to do balanced exchange but that you can't steal anything from me anymore, and in my mind the arched fucking that was feral and all fire becomes a pile of grapes, melting, stomped with kissing, and we are drinking everything softly, the liquid melting upwards into our brains, sleeping back down into pleasure, then back up into our brains again. That karma was exhausting, boring, wasn't working out for me, I'm done with it, but if you want to come get it, the love is always here for you. That is not karma that is just potential, divinity upon this sweet Earth I grasp fierce and unfold my fist and a flower is there.

I don't understand the vocabulary of this modality, I am going to say zero point energy from now on, I am going to say energy with integrity from now on, these binaries drop out.

*If woman had desires other than 'penis-envy', this would call into
question the unity, the uniqueness, the simplicity of the mirror
charged with sending man's image back to him—albeit inverted.*
— Luce Irigaray

Someone is bartering in the shower
    showering in the verbena
re-arranging the pronouns
    from the plastic hammock
no longer to be punished with attention
    but with purposive absence, and porn
slotted in to the empty place,
    porn with its
spoon from the kitchen
    porn with its
fork in the mustard
    with its pencil shirt
lasciviously
    sexist with its
woman with a sexist face
    ruling by gavel. Why
is no one reincarnated as a pigeon

        leaping and sedition

done always from far away.
    Considering how and when we are
going to admit our love of manufacturing
    our genuine condolences re: iPhone
our joy exchanged for mourning
    I could hold on to
you could not pull back

        I could sully
you could Wednesday
        et cetera, either/or
pour
        from my garden
of singing, a punishment
        hanging from the neck
of a CHATTEL
        and if I say FREE
then so what
        what happened
is happening
        again
song—

From the alienated companions I had thought to call hipsters
I learn that the teenagers of today's generation
read periods in texts as passive aggressive,
that if someone says I'm late
and you respond okay
it's okay
and if you respond okay period
it's not okay—
and from them again I learn to be meat
and need a better camera
with which to mimic the surface

beneath which I fawn with industry.
The bottom of myself drops out
awake and charged by hashtags
seeking to decipher the difference between actress who fucks and
        actress who does not
                between fucking for pay and representing for pay
                between actress who is paid and actress who is not
                between actress who does not fuck and stand-in who fucks
        for her hierarchy
of petted morals which possess my body intimately

can I speak of violence with body intact
except you do not wish to hear it, will inspect me for wounds
every other enemy's a standing manuscript
every other manuscript who's enemy's a woman standing
a woman photographed in the act of excusing her patriarch
who happens to be a woman in a suit but it doesn't matter
it doesn't matter
actress whose body pleases dirty-shirt man
whom envy has bound to a couch—

Purported envy which flexes our fingers in dance of refute
The refutation of which constitutes more fully a defence of the
　　masculine
The refutation of which is necessary to the love of right
The refutation of which may be right, but not true
May be accompanied by a recuperation of the dildo
quartz, amethyst, rhodochrosite dildo
　　pink tourmaline dildo
shungite dildo
　　laughed at yr dildo over lunch dildo
dildo of fat art dildo of proof
　　of recognition dildo
　　　　　　proof that what begins specialized as medicine
　　　　flying out of left field
　　　　　　may end as daily practice
　　　　　　　　yuppie fetish dildo
how can I envy what I can buy with my wage
　　what redefines my status as sexual proletarian
how can I buy that

I used to believe that there was really such a thing as a woman with no
　　　　　　　　　　　　　　　　　　　　　　limits

　　the byproduct of a broken fantasy of community, perhaps
or just the long germination of stupidity and fixity—

The strap-on was purple, and decorated with daisies,
how pretending to have a cock is girlish I don't recall
    to numb the threat of my having it all
I suppose
    I thought it would extend the clitoris of my feeling
into the muscle, but I was wrong—
    without a daisy chain of jism to entice an ending
the only point of a strap-on is to make someone wail
    the weapon stripped of its empathic sweetness
is just a weapon, is this what it's like
    to be envied

My belly pops with stars where they put the needles in so I crush myself
                                 into bed, ears popping with wheat
and oatstraw, crush the yarrow beneath my shoulders, grappling with
                                 an obscure wrangling I still can't
vocalize, it is a rock I am inhaling, hoping to improve my life with
                                 enough cash to pay to spray
paint my body with golden sun, to spray paint my naked body with
                                 naked golden sun, and retreat
to the bedroom at night with the dancing bears and console myself
                                 with a decoction of tears—

this rock I am inhaling is gold in my mouth—all of my rocks are gold.
Gold falls out of my bra when I stoop to pick up the gold
that fell out of my hair. My skin is gold, my fingernails, ideas
are gold my refusal is gold, my refusal is gold, it goes
from rock to gold to golden, the path I am walking
      along is golden, light that falls
along it golden, grass is golden,
garlic-tops are golden the odyssey we
just ended is golden the conjuncts are
golden the work is golden the needles
are gold the seeds are gold.
      The clarity is
golden is the one I am writing for, the flame
is golden is the night I am writing in
the day I am crying in is golden
golden, golden, golden,
the woman, refusal, rage,
and righteousness golden, the sage
I smudged the door and car with
golden, with what I endured

a lion devouring the sun
golden a lecture about suffering
and silence golden, a gold
pear mixed with salt and honey
and yellow lemons—the missing is golden,
the hatred is golden, the healing is golden,
the healing and healer are golden and gold.

The transformation is
not golden but leads to gold. The
vast fields of infirmity and disastrous
oppositions.
Competition is lifetimes
of servitude, but
rewards without boundaries
are not limitless.
This should end up looking like a kind
of logic, although is precisely what I
dismissed yesterday,
the end of days.
The future is now, divided by sleeping
divided by energy and information
into attention and focus
into an undivided path we are walking
not separately, not together, but as
one motion forward.

WORD/WORLD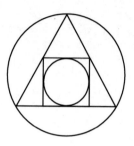

When dwelling in the dark. The painfulness either of
a bear paw waving over a stuffed hump, or the audio
mixing with the moan of a deceased child
actor whose fearlessness was childish. Terror
not in explosions but hearts
who defend hearts against hate
calling hate a kind of love.
The girl says conspiracy theories make her try not to hate humans
disclosing the limit of her patience, and
a man's love of bears is revealed as autism,
who can insist upon knowing anything,
how to get up.
I remember giving
up along an axis of origins, a dull planing
of grief that it should be so
difficult to walk through a palate of rot like it's nothing. How some
                                                              filters allow
a person to hide from an ugly world and believe in beauty and how
                                                                beauty
is the result of a long built and painstaking wildness, or neither.
A lightness in atoms
isn't enough
protection. There are these words like civilization.
People say a word like flag. I pick my teeth
high up in the hills.
A person can rise
through the weight of a smog of words
or exploded oil, where ears
and lungs take the bait.
Steel world, a bolt through my ear.
Asphalt world, cloth in my mouth.

But how uncanny that I should be pressing 'stop' on the grizzly
                                                    bear DVD
just as a grizzly bear documentary is beginning on the BBC.
Our integration left us clueless
about everything except the private miseries of an adventure team,
knowledge subject to the passage of time. We're not
together, we know ourselves apart, apartheid of beasts.
Is it animal half interested in food
or a mothering instinct we might share.
Bears get shirty, do whatever, a rising tide of consciousness
is shirty and/or sensitive, the weather and chemicals
flow in. Then someone adds narrative,
tugs away on feelings. Then you die chemically,
someone sees dragons in the sky.
In real life they are divebombed by eagles
and I walk saying I believe
in something beginning with mal
and holding dolor in a pall
when he's murdered and the justice
only depends.

The fronds of late summer went away today except one
which is pale without companions, dark companions
have their pinions stuck on others.
                                        Weird charitable
inversions flow out of them, veterans peel the day
for opportunities, then get in. Looking at what
I think I am and then what I am, what simplicity
I can forage out of manage to ambulate, speak
clearly, animate,
clearly animate
a fantasy about cleaning the floor with
a heavy reliance on the hip flexors, imagery
heightens tension in silver grey in PVC
I blend the trousers and drink them,
they are "mine", in 1970.
But today, the apple core
of all history is how we reserve our taking-
out for a special one to call home, swallow
bitters with in the evening with,
and the units shall henceforth spring forth alongside,
to busy ourselves with neutral marriages and
general fucking, was pleasurable because
we were all together, talking, and
working things out, and no
'honour' was cowered at by imaginary women
who were actually real, and did cower,
no men selling and buying, and pointing
and buying and selling, and pointing
their fingers and selling, and pointing
their fingers and lying, that
was not inherent
to man
or
to men.

Who made my men for example, a long
history of psychotic episodes,
in France they called revolts 'emotions'
when peasants did them, now my
tongue rests on free housework
and battles history
with death's stories, their
white fingers
bending to live best.

The worms quieten
in me for many days
then spray their heads up-
side down and backcomb the locks and then
be free of everything that once called
with its grandiose space, its nothingness
its parachute grapefruits and bruised blue
soap.
In the bigger picture, do we
have time for this, episodes
chronically doomed to fail,
men lined up to die
with their complete wage
solidified in petrol around them
in fire, in earth, in metal, in water, in wood,
and in plastic.
Now who are we why are we
here doing these sorts of things.

comes in right thinking, right thinking a mix of healing and devastation
when we full of easy food sat and listened to Winona LaDuke
calmly documenting the crop murders and the line
between heritage and farming. The state insinuates itself
into the land and says how and what you can grow. The reason
they call it an heirloom seed
is because it's family, but
there's no such thing
as right thinking
if it's true we eat our guilt, and a plastic seed can be
made to feed
a brittle world
until
our bones give way and then
drop down into pleasure called
running away, a dull storm riding out its place between my eyes.
I asked the university what "post-colonial" meant, but
they only wanted to talk about the texts.
So you learn that learning is a regiment, and go
put body in mind and then go rip them both through blood.
When my friend says there is a pure
violence and a structure that is violent and that
one is more, and I don't know how to disagree with my mouth
with the wrong that surges through all violence
on earth, that the most recent is the worst.
I think a shop is barbaric
when it won't refund me.
Which is grief without ownership
floods into the morning with its wakeful song
bathed in men, and blood, and theft
and now women too
their remains in their hands
covered over a camera
roaming a food supply

unparalleled on earth.
Having inherited the earth
no one is meek in the aisles
no one is meek in the parking lot
and jawed heads protect
the poverty of imbalance
because they tell us it's balance and
words
are
spells

ALPHABET POEMS

This entire seascape black, black,
Black back holed competition of absurd trumpet sounds.
Absurd trumpet sounds wants to hold my hand eventually, finally, after
Finally I am sick of joined skin and just want to gnaw on my face in a
room alone.
That is how to join skin.
Refreshed by the alterity of the space between us
Into which the emotions goes
by halves because we are sharing it and the plants so much.
Trembling with the weight of our lungs and feet and quivering trembling
and when I
Cry holding the dog I fear I'm putting something on him
Other than the quaint diamanté splashes of tears
Like the heap of tears that was paper that slumped beneath the
campus billboards
And which disappeared overnight
I'm taking notes about nothing, everything. All the stupid things that
Creep in between how I feel about the day and how the herbs affect me,
How the sprays take us home, where we await the arms of favourite
people,
Our stress melting or burgeoning and in either case taking us with it
Yes we, all of us, at the bar, café, conference, gallery, library, office,
orgy, party, seaside, weekend.
This thisness of I am a boat,
This reclamation voyage, the blood from which I can crow but do
not come
Of getting not off
Of the do coming again
Of not to do come again
And do again when I think of it
A blood voyage
Embarked upon by the burgeoning mood I've drunk

TO

Sit on me, I've reached that age now. Sit on my gun rugged. Age.
I'm at the age where a cobra is inoffensive to any spread-legged warpath
And the double oblivion upon which my very existence depends in our
Eyes is just burnt in the fire, and we move forward, that's we as in I and
I when we're jointed like a bull to his yoke and it's
Elasticity and brimstone and the inability to countenance
Any slapping parasol in my ear or parasol tooting lower than ear level
Because I'm not going to stoop to reach and I want
Even to sink lower, so the threat of helmets is rendered extinct by
Its happening on my head, with wings, plumes of roughened steel
Inebriated with unexplainable lightness
Where I want to dismantle everything that is not a tree,
Fists and knuckles anthropomorphised so I can raise them,
Raze them down to dust, make ashes of them to smear
Upon the fearful god who is my boutique surprise confidante in the
                                                    shroud of crime

Shrouding
Around the safety of home I want to write, when the key's melted.
And when the key's melted,
Someone will come out in
Maybe dripping eagle feathers and distract you from your
Set of worries, evacuate you
Skyward, heap you up like wet food
A mammal plaining for some
Distances that cannot be traversed, simpletons
I am a row of thumbs, each one a simpleton,
Choosing to turn one up or one down, down one
Sweaty row of condoms, chowder
The imprint of immigrants on your border
How I brought all this excrescence and the crescent within it
Turns it into growing, which is what I do
And I step upon the flowers I can't name
Bougainvillea actually
I can identify correctly

26

FREE

I want something to soothe me but nothing will so so what
Complaining about poems
Today I walked extra blocks from the store to the other store
To make the journey for early tonic that was necessary
And found myself caught between a rising moon and a setting sun
The one fat full, the other gauze gold, embattling
The entirety of the back sky. Goodbye.
Out into the back of the past,
Back's traumatic grasp.

It is not arguable that ideas have consequences.
But the rub is the choice of the word. "Consequences". It is a
Clever word. Do you not think. Or something.
Can I get off. Want to get off.
Want to get off.

All that I wanted
To say I would say. All that I wanted
To say I would
say, late in the game and would
Say, say it anyway
Way

What if the rhythms were uninterrupted?
When I takes it away, then look,
All the poems are I made up.
All the beautiful controlling bullshit
Upon which I also am feeding my nosebag, but
Behind my eyes, a serpent
Fires the coals.

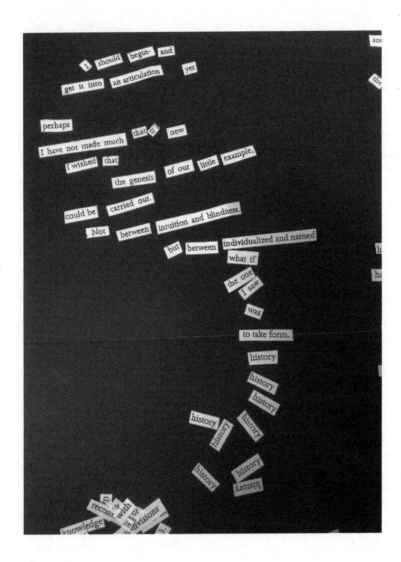

1 This poem is a cut-up of the Foreword to the English edition of Michel
  Foucault's *The Order of Things*

FIVE FLEE WITH SWORDS AND TWO REMAIN BEHIND

In this one he's made off with the lion's share
But it is the little remaining lambs that bite his gullet
Hug him in the guts where he can't feel. The triple
Salamander sky opens its stomach and turns out
A tune, a tuning fork, a pitchfork, a forklift
Singer who does me up a melody tune. As girls
We are talking on the phone in a little bit of love
Shyly merging with staying, hoping rope
Will turn our necks and insist upon
Knowing as an other world's thing.
Strap on the periods of time and grammar
With moony lows to the high point of
Your day, which I promise not to ruin
This time
Although I know I ruined it last time.
What use is any form of regret
If it pertains to anything back in that
Past there
Pear between my mouths
So I can play to read the symbols
Even in what I do not act upon to gather
Together we are unwilling
We are forging make-up in our hand-mirrors
We are doubling up the words and
Pissing on those
Upon whom we will not sit and spin Isis
Into milk red legs, she goes
Hurt and gasping, papered
Unaware, collected, papered
Slack, hoisted, papered.

In my bowl: 5 ants
                  1 spider
& the refusal of an injured cat

Would have to make its exit
undramatically just bleed out. Into the warm water
holding the sloughed off remains of these various.
Attachments by wires to desire in its several forms
of whom I list towards waiting, around my waist
a band of idleness tightens and talks to me drapes
me in bugs who know the weak spots and seek
them out who lick me in my weak spots
no intention of their own. It is a
distance seeking, a redness humming,
a bird thwarting my sense of its blue
by racing. Hopefully
this will be one more minute through
which I can last. Hopefully
a sense of me wilts late enough to keep her memory
stanching the genetic drizzle
I willfully choose
to go back to the fake stone land
with its swirls of gold fabric
its renditions of hilarious promises
its accusations against
my perpetual nothingness.
Stupidity I willfully choose
to dandle upon my sugared knee,
cup its face and say baby. But the
Poem is called SEX so what do you want
but I gave you Isis in the last and will give you
a bowl of fresh cut irises now so
be satisfied.

FIRST HEAVEN

How I promised
NOTHING
How I
NOTHING
And cupped a cupcake butt instead
And thought to hell with learning meaning
When there is bread under my fingernails
And as the saying goes
To pluck art from off the brave air
Complete helpless fad. Refute nothing
Only do what comes.
Fast when I have stopped
The frying and the slotted spooning
Heaped
The onions through my vitals crimped
Only the resultant memories, real estate
Agents I've attracted somehow managed to cull me
Anyway and push me into financial carrots
I chase, shitting opals like back in the day I did
And no one would stop me, wresting
The truth from its dictionary
And nestling it in my inflated lavender bra
Saving me not for later but forever as wishes have horses
Sun-drench the pitiful pitfalls of sky and meat substitute.
The minute I begun negotiating with coherent effort
Was the beginning of the end, the gun, the years
I sat at the computer watching songs take many hours
To download. Blue, blue,
Nothing tastes so sweet as you.
I'm gorging on my own corpse. From the moment I wake up.
Before I put on my make-up. It's in us right now, I said.
I was referring to death. It's amazing
That we're alive at all, I said. Isn't it amazing?

He may have grunted, if I were to have streamed rainbows
Out of my unicorn butt in the sunlit garden past sundown
Which I do almost every morning, scrumming his
Warm ears with my muzzle.

HATE

MINE

Taking out the damage of red
By scrubbing it out with gold again,
        gold again

and papering over the bits
cut in haste

Dear psycho when the moon[2] shines

2 shady green moon

I am afraid
Of eating one it's been some time since I have been eating one and
                                        the hip.
He did crap sleep and then pushed one out with his lips puckered
                                        like ass.
Hike my face up to the unsatisfied fantasies that come to imply running
As a breaded certainty or the flap tones ripped in gold then burnished
                                        then
Tossed away into a flint of diffidence which glows hot pink at its tip and
Sags in black and then eventually shrivels, like sucking off a
Bowl of pasta instead of one's true love moved through.
Soaped a pleasure imagined it reeked. It was like
A dog crimping. It
Built a fence around it and tugged its humps.
It was flat and collegiate, metempsychosis in the night.
It was trapped between the plastic and the rug and no one
Was going to tell you otherwise because you knew,
You knew. You knew. You knew.
You always knew you
Sausage plain. You
Morning looking for a scrap and finding a woodpecker.
You around whom the magic tourists gathered you
Around whom the pen wrapped its fingers you
Around whom the vulva of great magnitude imposed certainty you
Around whom future curdled and turned into a dairy product
You who dreamed against me and died far apart you
Buried in the land you who wasted by degrees
Of truth and untruth. Lo and the forest opened its sky and
Lo demons came unfurled from out upon putting it right.

A trap like
Composition which creates evasions of space dread
The homecoming fervor torpor turgid leaf throttle
Me against the headboard in the tent like a sex
Which you put on me some time ago, the numbers
Continuing their ornery arbitration, the
Legal sparks tuned up to blimps that pump against
Robins, bluejays and
Some other smaller birds, manzanita I'm here but
Dwarf shrub it didn't matter how late
To the game
Out
To the sky
And a cradled confession that curdles
That warms the stuck pig part
That wasn't let's be honest all so very much hurt.
But it's the same for us all, all of us
Feeling the tension in the tendons.
That was a hurt built up and that was a shriek owl
Was a camp manufacturing bombs and plotting late-night howls
One was a trust thing one was a rainbow visitation.
Either way, clammy in the night, thinking about purposeful
Activities. And the suds shake. And the prayer hands hum
Their inevitable collapse. And the drinks take.
And we're going on walks from a place that we drive to.
And the numbers are right, so, well. The numbers are right.

With the goddess and a small llama, whereby our
Drawbridge bows back and our bodies bow low
To kiss the feet of our own bodies and the natural
     hair of the soil grass
And in all of our kissing a small trail of lowing
And in all of our lowing a small trail of knowing
From the hands that have loved there before.

Something of darker mettle, they said. They requested.
Something of darker mettle. Them and their
Wants. Of organised mettle. Fuck you! I said.
Poured frayed panties from the broken neti pot into
The almost empty but resealable bag. Her earth hands.
Bag like I am.
A month on the lips, seventeen years in the hips
The holding-in sounds. The slipping-in sounds.
The groans, loaming archers, swoop low. I know
Them and a plastic container of oiled nuts.
To stop biting
At my own lips
For eighty dollars and a vial of my salt
Which I will replenish with the fat of something dead
So I can eat. A row of exes: x x x x x x x x x x x x x x x x x

FORTITUDE

Strength to be
slipping through a potato mood like this. This
one potato mood, two, counting on me for us
strangulated supper penance. Flipped
and it was just me alone thinking about an itch
of vague purport, deep in the
et cetera, curdles
my day into perishable exactitude
how I waste as one soaks hay in the
savagery of working for pay, a one how I need,
a two how I distribute
my plaints evenly among the day
plan to evacuate vases otherwise full of me
petulant, rubber-wrapped, pink balls buoy my arms.
Which is to say, dreamt
in the nights of these crying women, our arms
extended across oceans of immutable undulant
seeds sown in time to break
me hate me and downed neck
I am ruffling the blue cuffs with a pearly paste
pretending for hours that I'm not
what I say I am
not,
                           thanks to the table
between slips in my meaning
I can be permitted to explore
anything, anything

His house makes wildness in the hair of women, imagine
at her desk dumbed down putting the wrong conjunction in
to the washing machine and swivels instead of spins oops
is coerced by the sheer volume of recklessness
that one will spin in return for payment and nod
to the official standing of pay and its sturdy purple
sky, gloomy in the back of us
and this is my front, a natural downturning in the
shouts for me to get out, blank foreplay of sponsorship
to haul my media from her galley to the phone
and back down again to a seeming absence of artists
from up in the top floor of the building which is
not earthquake-proof, repeats
its flimsy bendable status. Low exhale it seems
so much unlike what I need
this darkness, apparently

Who in her disembodied carnival heeds no thirsty imperatives
Of years teeming into bodies hooved at desks
Rubbed off on the carpet our animal ways and cried
Me in my shame! My hooves became
Carpets of shame laid beneath strips of light I peeled lace off the page
To make space for my practicing emptiness
Hoping a thinner book would appease the past
Throwing out years of humped scrawls on knees
Crawling around the parameters of investigation
Which are the limitations of imagination
To strop politely hiding and throwing up
My hands into books, believing if I love
Them and rest my head upon them lovingly
The paper will automatically disintegrate the knowledge
Pour unfettered into my head

Dear people, why
are your company ruining the earth not
our kind in a coach bag sequestered bag
bagged up in a bag of bags, but for all the bags
outwards from the face, they are slurped up and stitched
up. I repeat, why are you ruining everything
to save your company because it's the future
of all my retreats they say happily. In my
best interests. A stack of Sports
Illustrated I was dying for.
A pastel diorama of aerobicized
thighs wrapped in alien snakes I was
dying for, and hunks
of gold at my ears I was dying for.
Napalm as analogy for
what microwave does to food, and for
how anything can be borne upon. At night the word
domestic floats in upon a sea of particles,
and how else are you supposed to make
this kind of friend, we are going to
have it all
a rhyme, a rim, a rip, a rape, a parade,
and a fantasy of public speaking
that is a movie by Universal Pictures
that is a political fantasy about planting
trees that implies that if we keep planting
trees now and then that there will be
seas of soft fluffy trees instead of capitalists
once again as soon as the fetish for soft sweaters
dies down
but the fetish for soft sweaters
will never die down nor the Dow die
down low enough to crack
in my balloon head stapled to reality

one nub at a time removing my unofficial
tempestuous return to exceptional
living which is an eventual poverty
an eventual desperation
a hurt about hope, an encouragement
about lifting, a promise about
payment it is always in this
mode a choice about consumption
the visual echo of a squirm
a trap clapped down
upon the head of a dog

Saliva burnt to an acid thought. How hardness
comes to rule its roost exhaling into the space
between my ribs melanotic with sun crazy sun
crazy sun crazy sun order slow sun crazy order.
How to do opening to do softening when hard
is the day's rule rote cellular. Pushed me for
example into the back of my heaving up tears,
their rocking obliterated in sweltering ribbon
absence has fangs to make me feign knowing
the future creamed into gallery posters stitched
and dampened and solar-powered. Honey my
socks are wind-farmed. There are no appropriate photos I feel
reflect my oneness now. Drop
a few licks between pixels, whatever, pickaxe
to drop me down through the chair and my
costal balloons make a bellyful of calm I am
who I am who I am is this rinsing
measure along the chart of the certainty of death
beginning to have happened alongside me
all I want is a shaved fish. That is it is the
order of everything out of joint. I have these
magnets in the base of me but I belong
in the moving dark the ripping clock I'm
buried in the moving clock the ripening
the rings of iron around necks, wrists the
rings of diamonds around necks, fingers
the calm inevitability of order I plan
to smudge it into my own forehead deepest
daunting destination I crawl against

Imagine. Imagine. If this were like social.
Construction. There.
Would be a door. Then.
People would walk through it. No why
Must there be a door. If there were no door. Even
If there were no door. There would be a perimeter.
Maybe it would extend to the port. Maybe not. With no
Door who is it's to say. If this were like social
Construction. There would be stops. In strange
Places there would be decisions that were totally arbitrary.
ἀγεωμέτρητος μηδεὶς εἰσίτω[3]
There would be fisticuffs and bloatings. The poem
Would swell in
Unfortunate
Pla-
Ces and then tighten again uncertainly. I would become its parents
Allowing a shady mix of ethics and egoism to colour my
Methods probably
The aim of which
Broadly. Would.
Be to either stop the fonts of crying or
Turn on the. Fonts.
Of crying.

3 Ageōmétrētos mēdeìs eisítō. "Let no one untrained in geometry enter."

Entry was permissible by heart but not
paper. Because I neglected the paper. Because I let the song
die down among
noises and calendars
whose width and duration expand irrationally
taking our time snatching it up cooling off. As if
the codex were inflatable, lifting immeasurably
into what community suggests and demands
upon time. Upon the notion of expanding
around 360 degrees, that is
what the heart does, and then
contracts again
endlessly mugwort
to engulf sleep, but will it
be more than plain longing
tread watery space my books
my muscles my thoughts hover
hover.

Is hanging in the air. I suppose I may have done this or that
thing under the influence of things unbeknownst to my
sense of control jasmine. You know now how you
are repeating the leash by becoming unaware
of ideology which is both in life and in art a suck bag.
Then if I say suck bags again as a proper noun against dinner
it will search out most unlike lights to prepare us for a
talk about bombing which we do not have time to attend.
Then it's between his or her fingers and pushing into his or her
side. Then it's interesting because there was blood, and because
the rights of man and or woman were by implication at stake.
And then in modern times we can turn ourselves around by
exploiting these old systems. Our ironies are plangent harps
murdering the droning of our accents. I will just
look for a new one, a snake slipping through the floorboards,
an accident that no one will apologise for. I who run
the sagging rehearsals around history with no time to attend.
I who compete but drag about the heels, or float like
a child ghost, slow and luffing for the open fridge
I glow behind, in the eyes. How this is not apparently
going to be organisable by genre or martyr. How apparently
any old thing with enough questioning behind it.
Can come and soap me in the tub. How the day
crisps its edges like eating out. How waste is
fear of separation. How everything is running out
when it ought to be reinstating.
The ground dries up and they can't imagine that there
is water.

How we laughed
at each other
when each other
did what we did
when we did a stupid
swipe at ourselves
in bad mirroring
inverse doubling
carsick gaming.

A bird
kissing the heart out
of its prey.

You and I are supposed to be objective
in our merging, touching
clamping, wearing
our uniforms to present ourselves
first with language then with fist.
In any given context cull what is privilege
if you can spot it to cull it to begin
with.

When we present ourselves to each other
and there is no language beneath us
words rip away to tears
worlds rip away the memories.
I used to be incisive only in absences
because I was too sick to choose
now I hunger, anger
for hope, for humility.

EMPTY STREET

This is
how weather makes long times seem longer and
other times seem lost
to the drizzle of sky, the low overheads
the offhand remarks about travel, the radical
chic money flowing through,
laziness is fear laziness is psychological tugs
at my sense of having horns to toss brightly
sense of myself dissolving into "who do we think we are".
After the culling
when the world dies down
and things again sprout and run wild and go uncontained
and are not sold to nor sold on nor soldered to
a sound like cash
we will
hurtle to
wherever

PLENTY MORE

He who bendeth like a vulture over me in a song of bending a swarming
down of honeysuckle into my nose doth tear me from purity, my ground
of being touching the earth in a variety of poses, their love easy
when remembered easily forgotten. The nose of warmth that draws
any creature away from him her presence in a coffeehouse, reality

beckon

at the bottom of a great height of trees. The treeline, horizon, hilltop
cradles and accentuates the dipping of stars we are planning to
rush home to shave, a thought on which my cradle sticks. To
find and rush into one of a mind of the planting of seeds
and to a one whose not being whole notes of desire planting
into a score that vibrates. How many ways I can put
this desire's path of war, all of its tugging begs
to be rendered language. To waste us. These pure beings who fuck
excitedly imagining
forests of infants in seed gardens springing
forth from the berries of their loins. This Aztec
purity not even Aztec or anyone's, cedar nuts
purity that sequesters no one in a concrete structure to suck
money from the corporal vein. Whose hands bear cloth
bear down upon a dance, claws retracted strategically
missed her when her absence grew fundamentally apart
but do not want to hear them again
their taking themselves away with great excuses
their bright ideological spots
no clay can scrub out. Sit
with me here upon
a piece of the Earth
to begin again

IT FITS

It jumps about
a giant
leg stepping across the earth
it slings
its
pelvis like
a team.

APPLES + ORIGINS

#1, THE HARD MOON

One who tumbled out done. Not true.
Truth of emotions gone through, first
bodywork run through, rescinded betrayal
of broken young body, who knew no
name to call in closeness. A withered bird supped me
everywhere, across the city and room
feet slapped feeling across the gate.
The date he arrived in my room it was good
to be a vessel of permission in a blue silk robe,
because my hair frames my memories,
a girl born to parade and a men of church army.

Slippage on the road, supposed to be tread.
I slip now thinking, it hurt him to be left,
slip back into thinking, I started out that way,
the difficulty of feeling,
        grab my
persimmon, it rhymes with permission, hook into my wrist
my lab coat splits
its lips. The days I escape.
I am in the dirt looking for worms.
I am wrapped in polyester, sad feel of kids' clothes,
I am sitting at the table
broken into my food, my drawing exercise,
admissions of things, not sure I did them,
night-time screams, flying things,
buckled pews, outfits, terror terror.

A liquid comes up and is swallowed.

Pretty
at this point but
        still the hard moon. I feel in accordance
with sense, a

cloud of starry imminence
makes him remember me,
whoever he is.

It's hard to write, the sops in their repetitions,
electrolytes kicked
through ether, land in shoulder, land in throat.
Land in shoulder, land in throat,
spray consciousness aerosol.
It was just circumstance,
how we used to wake under white sky, no trees.

The hard moon again, going to bed
as I am awake in the world,
and there is an ancient
unknowing that I also followed deeply
by its little red rope beneath the world.

Things I might take for granted: a trine
of Earth and Moon. What does it mean
to hang yourself on a hook,
or to live in what feels like water,
needing Earth? What does it mean
to grow up permanently slapped.

I learn that everyone I trust will be dangerous.
                    They threw me
around the room, hitting what bounced with a brush,
hostage
to soup can smacks in a language they wrote,
but it were stupid, and I are clever,
and in the basement I have
the top floor office, and there is a star across the windows
to the sky.

They do not want me to be safe
except from the world
confined to a region
of long purple bruise-clouds.
Have I remembered her recognition,
or did I download it there after?

To learn
to love
your
self,
know
a shadow
is there

saying it
is a cognition
that opens,
to say—
with all of my love I will not do this anymore

There were things I wanted to ask, like,
now that I have a picture of the angles and planets and know
that it was hard not just because I thought it was but because
the angles are actually called hard angles,
what kinds of power can I mobilise in service of Earth?
Via quintessence of MOON, a glowing mist calls
my head back 180 into sky on a Monday, impressed
by much rain.
Where are my permissions, I
am too young to know them, I
say them with cells shut, I
cannot be read like a book
precursor to a spread wing, an opening—
forcing the door was just imitation
of a method tried on me: BUT NOW I SEEK THE END
OF REVOLUTIONS OF THIS KIND. THE DEAD
CALL ME. IN MY KINDNESS
I SUBSUME VIOLENCE
WHAT IS TIME IF NOT A QUEST, A RIPENING,
A LIGHT THAT CONQUERS EVERY SHADOW, AND
REPETITION IS DULL.
Do you really want to hear it all again? Do
you want to hear any of this again? Cough
up a little ball of shadows.

All these thunderstorms consciousness.
An afternoon tidal thing
I clamped my arms around grandmother. A bird
a yellow bird a yellow bird
envelopes the sky a yellow sky
how I held you how
the days are decreasing how the angles are slimming
how the season is season of death

open my head words come in

How harpooned. How a harpoon holds. Let's get right to it—
will let me go once I've said it all.

How harpoons hold hope hostage, I am a great whale
harpooned in a religious experience of martyrdom
and I am six, I am grown. The world is to be
carried on my orphaned body, seems right to be so.
I wanted to write it, heard it gear churned, then
felt abstracted by ordinariness.

I want the cone to come out of my solar plexus again,
I will do anything,
they say a lot of things,
like "words are spells"
and so I scratch out every thing I ever said
about any of it,
how the entire being of someone I loved insulted me
in every part of my body—
a tapestry, piece of work, going-through, absence,
complication, mirror, a body in her space, full of space,
all of time, time they hit her in front of me,
time they grabbed me in front of her,
time he raped me in front of school,
time she was the third point in a
triangle of abuse, whoever she is.

Persephone takes my hand, she is mother, she is deep red
winter glamour, she is a real estate agent but
also she is free, to roam the frozen earth barefoot in a peacoat—
What do you seek, she asks,
A new way of seeing, I reply, it is what I always reply and why
certain ordinary things are like being punched in the gut.

Violences I literally can't unwind from felt-sense,
an octopus around my head, starfish around my ankles,
sitting in a cup of coral, pink orbs revolving, tapping
the floor for kindness, tapping
the skin for sensation, the points for reprogramming.
I never looked so perfect as the time with the octopus around my head
except perhaps the time it wound around my legs,
around my arms or breasts—
it's not magic, it's energy
a term they forgot as they marched through the square
as they ran her out of town
and the tape gnarled
and the time to be open closed.

No amount of magic
to make me free: pineal gland, tibia,
sacred geometry, points on my ears, head on my
shoulders, seat of my relaxation,
actor in my animation—all pale
beside the indoor girls I have been—

The mystery of intention is that it only works
sometimes. But
when I was most frequently to be found dressed as a
severed pair of wings I was not also awake per se.

Let your tears
be a kind of wedding,
you go home when it's over.
The nights like nails,
puncture my skin like quills, from the inside, and now
I want you to pay me to do it to you.

Perhaps there is something in a history of categories.
How can you love being wolfed at when
IT IS YOU THAT IS WOLF

Sometimes when I am really fed up
I imagine that things will be different if I
can convince a stranger to let me fuck them in their car.
Then I imagine a tongue like babies, and
a wild, vulnerable wonder, and the cells'
breathing magnified, and it might be too much,
I might have to exclude myself from the rhythm permanently
(I say as if I have not already done this excluding
/ considered the sky /

       ran the gamut of persecuted stances /
tossed the foil gauntlet /

                      bounced / burned /
                    held a deerling in my lap /
was that small thing / was that broken small thing)—

Once upon a polished rock within a youtube sun
whose pink glow rises and falls a beautiful
woman tells her special story of being guided
by signs and through wildness to
a capitalist business model.
Estés and Myss were just saying that
being guided by signs and through wildness
means only that your heart is beating. Would you run
out into the street to scream, my heart is beating?
Because of course you are guided
by signs,
you are always on time.
What called me to follow you, or to garner being followed?
A deep force of change spoke in you, but
everyone is doing those trips now,
crawling the ruins,
leaving the garbage,
believing the website,
thinking a shaman
is something
outside of themselves that a price
will elicit inside of themselves,
but shaman is a word
several thousands of years after it is a man
with a need for quiet, for journeys
to the sky, for ecstasy, for joy alone,
and shaman is a word
several thousands of years after it is a woman
who hears the mountain shake and
feels herself within it, who feels the snake
awaken in her belly and helps it rise, who
blissfully cleans the floor. Your
very recent capitalism cut
down the trees, so

what do you expect, and you
outsourced the cleaning, so what do you expect. You
feared the snake, the dirt, you wrapped
your trash in plastic and assumed
it would transmute, what do you expect. The
mountain they moved to accommodate
the trash is
the step you seek, shamanically, othered
to a land where trash just disappears
you suppose.
It is not just your
West
stretch
pose that makes you feel like lying,
it is now also
the eradication
of the Mother place you came from, the Mother
you expect will clean up after you
forever. And when you try to reclaim her, you
become a tourist, not from anywhere, buying
the clothes, burning
the resins. But look, I know you cry
at night, I know you die
inside, I know you lie
in bed and let the terrors sink
deep into several pools of water at once
and wake into something
you've never known before
and no one applauds. It is the
energy you dwell in
of freedom, of yourself. It
is self-directed, green, not yellow—the
yellow part is for how and where
you trust yourself
to feel

The city opened to me, a white sky pouring green
tea over my vegetables. You
liked watching the liquid. I said I would
not be offended by any ideas, would reject identity,
would take responsibility for my energy,
and maybe that was the definition of health,
which you reject as a concept, which I critique as
misused as things always are trying
to catch the swallowtail edge of a thought, always are trying
to keep up, in the angular mattress slid between
being affected and holding on
to a thing I wanted
to say a rhizome
of tea and cups with tea in them, silty patronymic,
the difference between sadism and domination,
between misogyny and patriarchy,
between conservatism and compassion. I like
it when there are differences,
how hard you can pee when you're in your 20s vs
how hard you can pee when you're in your 30s,
between sick and well,
dysplasia, overdiagnoses, the
transition into somatic life,
the rejection of identity, the rejection of feminism,
the difference between the way I feel when I am
alone or not,
the information that creeps into me when I am still,
the things I did unconsciously meant more
than the things I did consciously, but what's
Freud got to do with it, it was spirit or it was matter,
one informing the other or the other acting headlessly.
A lost package returns.
An action married intention but after the fact.
I mastered myself so as not to be slammed shut

or made small, it turns out
it isn't about essential categories
of masculine or feminine at all

WHERE YOU ARE AT IS OKAY. GO FULLY INTO IT
BECAUSE YOU WILL COME OUT THE OTHER SIDE.

How far back the rape goes we do not know, except it may have
been the origin. An originary rape, with an unpronounceable name.
A long-held mystery, so originary that unknowing has come to feel
like knowing.

I dreamt of the song all night. All night it played in my dreams.
The force of it exploding through my fever, my intermittent peace
punched by its aggressions. Now I've caught its presence I can feel
it echoing all through my days and nights, like sonic chemtrails
polluting my ecosystem. These sparks that rise and go out. My
interpretations wish-based, corroded by hormones, influenced by
my belief in magic, starred by ritual. There are many things that
could be said to have ruined it, though it is tempting to say that
rape was the source of all ruin, which is why history is personal.

Still the song. It never stops. Seduction song. Direction
song. Song of masculine imbalance, which is feminine imbalance,
song of self, feedback looped into masculine imbalance, song of
romantic tropes practiced, unmeant unfelt. Song of performed
service, song to perform power, song to perform winning, song
to perform defeat, repeat performance, song of infamy posting
as comedy, song of battle in a soft field, song I love, song I hate,
song I jerk off to, song that triggers my longing uncomplicated
song that makes me feel the outline of something, outline of some
specific thing I thought I had and lost but never had, song / whose
friction was brief, song whose name I repeated, god and god song
whose thumb mashed my lips to my teeth song, stuffing dick in you
slow song trying to rip your track from your scalp song bitch song
deepest in you, sorry at the place where you cum from song you
cum to song you puff up your chest and be ego in song you pummel

bullies in song you cross the street in, blonde song who turns your head, blonde song who drives you home, man song who confounds you man song pussy dripping through your drawers song please stop please stop please stop please stop

Yes, a great wound, a many-layered multi-fingered wound I cannot name, only number:

1. Rape culture is still 100% in our face, so much so that it can be revealed only slowly and its veil may be made of gentle laughter and/or raucous indulgent repetition and/or subtle infamy.
2. Shame is a lie that we tell each other over and over.
3. We are divine, and our sexual energy is inseparable from our divinity. Sex is so commonly used to satisfy egoic desires or to distract from insecurities. But according to tantra, the alchemies of Horus, and the cult of Isis, the power of sex is to elevate and empower us, to charge our ethereal bodies with ecstasy, and to strengthen us against the forces that would turn us against ourselves and each other.
4. Sexual union that happens in mutual respect and love brings a state of surrender that creates a healing electromagnetic field called the microcosmic orbit which surrounds and nourishes us, expanding our presence and our capacity to give and receive love.
5. The empty space left by a lover is an outline of the infinite possibility of spirit.
6. If a lover is to serve their highest purpose they must take the infinite form, that you may dissolve yourself into it and be Not-you.
7. Men and women have ideas about each other, which they nurture in secluded spaces where they cannot be challenged, only reinforced.
8. These ideas create a behavior of expectation which draw out the mirror form they anticipate, first as an idea and second as an energetic possibility.

9. Love brings up all that is not like itself in order that it may be healed.
10. Love's agenda is not conquest, but ecstasy.
11. "It is important to notice what turns us on and to understand why it turns us on."
12. Sex profoundly alters the world. How we use it matters.

THE YEAR OF NO

I think I am done navigating the behavior of psychopaths
in order to suck more efficiently at the loop of his lip,
concurrently I release my psychotic self from its paraffin bag
of reproductive intent, and wake up to a sleepy
cloud covering the city, muffling our violent edges,
tugging violets through the holes in our skin,
like a cleaning that leaves everything intact
except see-through. But it feels cosmetic
to be done with a process
whose ghost is neverending. A death
of me is confirmed by a barn owl,
and an angel visits, but I go
on and wake up, into a world that is new
and a self more fully transparent.

I never knew what would happen
if I said "no" only that not saying "no"
was making it difficult
to be a person in the world.

I am courageous in my intention, less so in its execution,
to be free of certain kinds of discord, and I will banish you
from intimacy without boundaries
because ultimately, I want what is good
for everyone. And there is no such thing,
which is how you know I mean for myself
but myself is in service to the world.
Being a person in it

       I want the depthest most fundament
Mystery—
a particular space in which I can feel kind
of a transaction of kindness, a kind of
swapping of me in my room for me in my etheric room

for me in my selfie of etheric gloom
the guru in a certain kind of make-up
the way the water splishes
up the sides when a hip's bucket sways,
like navigating snakes, the questions
veer away as I veer away, into sky, into
moon, into stars, into foxlike, coaxful, whirring earth,
into compassionate, forgiving, white-glowing earth,
white-glowing woman on white-glowing earth.

DIFFERENT KINDS OF NO

Hers was a no that came out of a very long time saying yes

   Mine had been squashed

Ours was a no that came out of feeling yes, outside of thinking yes

   Ours was a thinking with feeling twisted up inside

Hers was a no that stood in the way

   Mine was a no that invited attention

Theirs was a no with a past

   Mine is a no with no past, only a fist

Mine is a no about trangressions

   They screamed theirs, I screamed mine, she screamed hers

We screamed ours, it screwed itself in

   Mine is a no that, under certain conditions, would be yes

Mine is a no that prepares the way for but does not necessitate yes

   Her no is social

My no is defiant, has a sense of self

Theirs is a no I don't want to hear,

      their heads' voices muted, easily neutralized,

largely shown on the surface, performed

Mine is a triumphant no, reestablished,

    exhausted

    by sentimental overtones of responsibility and coercion, sharp

    in my hip if left unsaid

Hers is a no uncertain, halting, brave, effacing

    fostered by seclusion, running from police,

    thwarted by sameness, uninterested in fashion,

    imprisoned but repeated, over and over

Ours is a mantra of sensitivity that through repetition

    emerges with wings that had been

    hidden beneath undertones and spreads

    above new walkways paved in skyscrapers

    walked by embodied dreamers

    whose lights look inwards, who compass

    passions, then blush outwards, like a spat

    word, into the rolled-up collisions

    of friends, of apartments, of dreams, of lovers

SATIATION, GRAVITATION, VIBRATION, PRIVATION

I finally, finally, figured it out
that power is about
where you put
the bed, the transformation
separate from what's happening in my head,
the rhyme I put on you,
the hyssop.

Why do I continue to believe in a paradise of trees
or a parade of wild grasses and its paramount
dance through wind, as if that could be
everything, caught between other less dramatic
less perfect moments more drudging more cruel,
more moments enslaved, more of us coping
with less of us, through a narrative
of too many.
I just want to be real two thumbs up from the bone,
I just want to be real like we were when we disappeared
into our bone-shaped bottle,
we are a generation who died
and set our wombs to seed, but we were men also,
did not have wombs, or had seeds, or had
a dogma ballet.
An entire genre
of clickbait
IT HAPPENED TO ME: I was
a useless assassin
because also empath
but they assigned me
anyway: in the future
they will know better
about Neptune
and they will send me away
to where to be without defenses

will be my absolute strength,
instead of how it isn't a strength at all,
instead of how not knowing how
to say no
is actually fucked.

Poetry is nothing, I saw a knife through my own throat,
and also it is everything, how the world types out
its rights and rules, under failed umbrella of law,
and written communication is a jawbone fence
knit with barbed wire and it stands between you and
the person you throw at it

a fence
guarded but see-through,
like I could see her whole entire house, when I was
supposed to see heart,
and the table opened up and ballooned out
and the tears took the air
into grace,
at the limit of what I can create—the man
talks about how our bodies will not take us into outer space
as I clutch the rabbit in my lap and beg him
to be a meat sack with me forever.

Ascension theory, you see
is for those who do not need their bodies
to be pummeled by survival trials—
for those whose bodies float on motorized
money clouds, mechanized
to reproduce effective
blinkers discourse
of what you can or cannot afford
to see or bear—

how every single moment is heaven, or hell
the twitter feed alternates between [genre] brutal injustices
the stomach of which rips heart out through its teeth
and [genre] instructions to create your own reality through intention
and have the struggle be over, or different—
how the discourse of spirituality
is a nice upper middle class whiteout
permitting exclusion from the harsh realities of industrial capitalism
a milky whitening, through which we ascend
to pretend that we don't have these meat sacks
to attend to
the amenities, the fuck-
ing
            AMENITIES—

And there is a difference between denial
and keeping myself like a temple,
to be reflective.
SHAMAN is crystal water, who dives and swims crystal-deep.
Or stands in a rigid, vibrating circle,
whose forcefield is permeable
and commands things out.
You can say no there,
in imaginal realms, outside
of material insults, a border.
So you say it, and hope that next
time will be different and
pull the drum tight and dive again

"Decide for yourself who you are and what you will create in your life and on the Earth, and then focus on that. Do not be drawn by the energies of anything that is not in alignment with what you wish to create."

The voice is here. I can feel its presence, its expansion in me, like a yes that buds from the root up through the trunk, blowing out into a gentle barrel, and flying up into the shoulders and neck. I dream of poking ink into my flesh. Requiring a city in order to find silence, to find the blindness that is acceptance, to find the letting go that is forgiveness, to turn my face into the sunny place propelled forward, to go always nearer to the source of the light. Because we know this is our last chance to live on Earth, and because we will not have another chance to go back again, in this life we cannot be distracted from our path. We do not want to go back with more questions pertaining to life on this Earth. We must learn them before we leave, loving every possible second upon this beautiful Earth, because we will not come back. We will move on elsewhere. It is like a heart breaking feeling suddenly, I see it all so clearly and I want this moment to stay. This feeling of certainty that the only thing that matters in this life is that you enjoy your time here and keep thirsting and seeking and do not resist the lessons, rush towards them and learn them all, so that you can die to yourself, die into light.

Please do not hate things, because in hating them, you hate. Please only love things, because in loving them, you love, or if you cannot love them be neutral about them, and remain in the truth of who you are, in the billowing, soft, strong energy of who you are.

The only way to destroy what we do not prefer is to step out both of it and the opposition to it. You hate the unfair thing, the evil thing, the hateful thing. But in hating it, you hate. It makes you hate. Step out of it. Be neutral. Be love.

Word/World
By Marianne Morris

First published in this edition by Boiler House Press 2017
Part of UEA Publishing Project
All rights reserved
© Marianne Morris 2017

The right of Marianne Morris to be identified as the author of this
work has been asserted in accordance with the with the Copyright,
Design & Patents Act, 1988.

Design and typesetting by Emily Benton
emilybentonbookdesigner.co.uk
Typeset in Arnhem
Printed by Imprint Digital, UK
Distributed by NBN International

This book is sold subject to the condition that it shall not, by way of trade
or otherwise, be lent, resold, hired out, stored in a retrieval system, or
otherwise circulated without the publisher's prior consent in any form
of binding or cover other than that in which it is published and without
a similar condition including this condition being imposed on the
subsequent purchaser.

ISBN 978-1-911343-21-9